NIG

HTIN

NGAL

ELE

SSN

ESS

GRAHAM FOUST / FLOOD EDITIONS / CHICAGO

Published by Flood Editions

www.floodeditions.com

ISBN 978-0-9981695-4-5

Cover illustration: Valentin de Boulogne,

Concert with Bas-relief, c. 1625.

Oil on canvas, 68 × 84 inches.

Musée du Louvre, Paris

Photograph by Thierry Le Mage

© RMN-Grand Palais / Art Resource, NY

Design and composition by Quemadura

Printed on acid-free, recycled paper

in the United States of America

I.M. / MWP (1969–2016) / MHH (1915–2016)

CONTENTS

As for the water of the fountain, it remained obdurately other,

singing mindlessly and unoppressed by time.

ANTHONY BURGESS, *ABBA ABBA*

NIGHTINGALELESSNESS

APPRAISER

What follows is probably at someone's expense.
(You now hear money spilling out from a piano.)
History was a mirror at a corner of the future,
and in fact, you can, from right where you are,
imagine consciousness, too, around the corner in a room
against a wall near the floor, and do your thinking there,
and so a plain, deliberate day does grade into a joy
almost unmoored from informations and their clamor.
This, in addition to the rest of your life, the life you lived
before we never met, before you set fingers and head
to skewed alignments of words, their depths mostly dim,
their surfaces seething, their shapes not much allowed
or just allowed unemphatically, as memoryless as cataracts.
But then you'd also turned them, the words, and hence
all that's in them—an interest in daylight, gardens,
and amounts; time always, love always, once more
with two feelings: the work of your discarded looks,
the scream of some small wheel that makes for speech.

Forever's a remedy, but as a remedy it's too easy.
(You once heard money spilling out from a piano.)

In the slick of any throat, there's much potential,
and yet with no great hope of impending understanding,
as full of calculations and arrangements as you are—
and damned if, having tested it, a plum in your hand
the way the sun's in a chuckhole, you'll forgo this view—
you know the closest you can get to you is meaning
not being mutual, but that there's some correlation
between world and having paid it any mind. Again
with this amateurish stitching, a symptom of sound
on your mouth and maybe others, a slag heap of sorts,
but recognizable, a few windows sheened in its dust
if you're lucky enough not to have worried too much
or so closely that you start to slowly vanish all day,
while over guy-wires, the stars like sand in bread, it all
(or in another word, nothing) keeps happening, newly cut,
yes, and as you won't have understood by then, not dead.

SENTENCE SOUNDS

(CENTRAL AND MOUNTAIN)

Oh. I lead off with loss again, the present
tense behaving the back way into the past,
that grand scheme of blooms and their moving too fast,
among which, unlikely, I lived and I don't,
my vantage points only the coast of myself,
an endlessly drawn-out sarcastic-ish kiss
at water making new pictures possible
and less, the days it rains and days it doesn't
trailing off into the record, the future
then ruining music for once and once more.

WITH

The natural place to begin is with
what amounts to our condition: glory
hallelujah, collateral Adderall,
collateral *quel dommage* along
the I-don't-do-umbrella Chippewa.
If the hinge of day can be called early,
we started early—hair of the dog—
and what we'd've given for a little tape hiss
to fraternize with, while the Enlightenment
tidied up our piles of mail.
This box that's made in ease's image,
we hear it out all year (e.g., a railroad tie
not quite itself among the flowers
someone's Photoshopped around it).

Got to bed last night same time same positions,
did some okay praying to the void.
Then woke away from there in shades the shapes
of flames or tall grasses, one stale almond in
each mouth or so it seemed and so it seems.
Now that we've improved all over everything,

am I, or are you, the sort of thing
that could be one of the many, or the few,
particular creatures in this world?
We like to say we hate the visual arts,
the ways adults address their children and pets,
the open sore or sewer we call the sea.
A single kinked leaf, still getting to be that way—
have at it. Or don't, because it's only not at fault.

THOSE MOUNTAINS, THAT BRANCH

To tell friend from foe in a novel
situation was the gods' job once—

when faith won't heal it lacerates.
what love can't want it breaks—

and since we've been left to just
those mountains, that branch

hung with trash, them battle apples,
hives of ovens, a couple turns

of sun, and one solid shoved into
another—since, that is, we've gone

all the way ape—it's like having come
back to a bad main idea, but also

to've sloped off home to have to think
of what our bones, bones mediocre

as anything else's—as everything else's—
would look like unattended to in mud.

FLICKS

No one in the movie hears the music in the movie.

×

Some rooms only *look* dark.

×

Slide a white tile beside
another of a different white,
and one will go near gray.

×

A spiderweb's dry lostness never permeates its spot for long.

×

A fly lifts off from a guitar string: song.

A LITTLE YOUNG FOR THAT

Shy joy
upon knowing what

some distant talk
or noise had meant,

and I forgot
to change even

the day back
together.

$$\times$$

To what end
would I wish to hide

evidence, live
happily?

$$\times$$

How I love
the gentle clobber of

the fool's gold of
the optimal;

spring's, too,
with its myriad

and multicolored
shrugs.

×

Unless
that's all it is,

some life's not
what it was

—like a train
unmeaningly

casting off
a landscape—

to see my own face
in any system.

ROILING BOIL

Before takeoff I say, "We'll always have oblivion. Again."
As opposed to that out-of-French-painting-looking cloud
or any other lovely failed attempt at chances for rain.

Some days you look like I think you don't see me,
and some days I look like I think you don't see me,
and some days it feels like a Sunday and it is.

Between too much not-enough and more than enough too-much,
we've come to what seems like an agreement, an order, but
it could be more like a flesh-packed maw lowering over us . . .

You know I don't need to be told that this ends uglily,
and I know you don't need to be told I don't need
to be told that this ends uglily, but we don't need

to just keep these things to ourselves now do we? Or do we?
Beyond word and number is a large body of water,
and beyond that body of water, still more water.

OLE MISS MOTEL

Sweat in the dish of the back of one knee, I kept quiet so as not to lie.

I watched the sky from the window of my unfamiliar room, but it was mostly as I'd known it, so I quit.

$$\times$$

It was someone's idea of a beautiful day.

The phone rang a rare and likely unbelonging ring.

Somewhere, one cigarette invented the air.

Infinity wasn't going to be much of anything.

WHEN I CONSIDER HOW MY LIGHT IS SPENT

I then change my practice from sport to war—
think, "The castle yells its wealth down into
the valley's vague plurality"; think, "To think
will on occasion lose its job"—and in the process
reach my current age, this very day, one end
of intuition. Mirrors shiver; aspens pixelate
the sky that lays the groundwork for the luck
of having stayed or walked away—to keep,
in either case, the pilgrim from the grave—
more frieze than film of pleasant desperation.
The rest is rain and epic narrative, is
and is not science—like falling fruit
or reaching (math or no math) up to pluck it—
and all that wishful grammar flashing back.

AMERICAN POET

Even calm breathing looks anxious on camera.

$\times$

Not everything you love's already art.

$\times$

To grayly shun all day
the sun's gradations isn't strange,

but you want words in an order
they were already in,

as if *that* were the thing
that must've been here forever.

$\times$

Scared into preparing,
you memorize with a hammer,

as if, having botched a torture,
you'd like your language watched.

$\times$

But what of life had you accepted more,
grasped faster; had you been more
the person you wished to be;

had you grown up farther with others, moved
by whatever you had reason to value,
loved ahead of time by whomever

first cared about an answer;
had you pledged to stop unloading
all that thought-work onto sleep?

×

In one quiet and emptily foreordained non-move,
you both dial up and phase out a feeling.

×

One thing leads to one
just like it.

×

If you think you've seen it all you've seen one thing.

WATER RIGHTS

Nights I *did* sleep, the quiet came right at me,
at which point I more than surrendered but worse.
First it came for the poet, and that didn't work,
so first it came for the would-be poet,
thus revising my slide into namelessness,
"the Chiefer part," that old sentimental fail-safe . . .
I dreamt up dead companions just to talk to them,
okay?—though light arrived and sopped up all we'd said—
and soon enough to be past all need myself,
I got up anyway, my each breath an "h"—
as if letters only smuggled meaning down
and into right now, the day and age that is,
or was, the phase I'm, what, the tinnitus of
mostly?—and tried hard to be without fail, toil,
or any irritable reaching after fact;
to think of life as the people who'd been there,
because life's all loss but isn't *only* that.
Not knowing death's an intelligence, I guess,
but one shorn of importance—no facts for us!—
like looking at something else and seeing clouds
or ink or some combination of the two,

all the worse to see me through to the future.
All hell coiled tightly, I haven't the faintest
what I'm keeping at bay, but I'm its expert,
inapparently, and the ever-backward shock
of a lack of name's the same all day, though it's
discrepant, too, like the difference between
a hand held out and a pan left out for rain.

TWO LAYOVERS

Animals caught, but released with the least of ease,
these birds in Terminal A've become a vague success,

a kind of comedy scraping its operative shape away,

while other creatures—those not lived with, really,
but rather vanished into, as when I enter the woods

as a deer or a wolf in a dream—are so much closer

than those beside whom I think I tread the world,
an anomaly halfway to ache what's there to have of them.

×

Having only now gotten around to that book on ambiguity,

the number seven on its cover like a scythe on snow,
the second person nominates its target and you're tired,

it's twilight, the sun's late work coming on like a word,

and so you've made a few mistakes, belief being but one side
of a screen or of a scream, the conditions against which

you wish to proceed seeming ever less clearly real in the light

of your love of the changeless and unnamed famous,
like that girl from Thrace who laughed down at wet Thales,

the heavens crammed duly with story but not one themselves.

TIME I'M NOT HERE

By way of days, I've moved as I've had to,
right on up to my past and never over,

and all day on all these days,
desires I wasn't to process washed in,

anxieties lullabied on
and quite liked to be gotten among,

but now—*and* now—one old,
abundant flower just screws up the room.

TRIGGER WARNING

There's an enlisted kind of prettiness
flaking away in these many places,
and it's like having been handed my hands,
this not-having-been-scared-enough-lately.
Germs leave worlds in me; flames close well-known roads
and even the seasons, immediately,
my failures next to language like a ditch
or sometimes in it like a bridge out, a trench.

On a good day, I fess up without remorse,
letting every formal model drift from dream
to near erasure; on a better one,
the grid willing, I lace my own and only
life like past affections, fled precedents,
gray light from some old film from some bad time.

DIMINISHING RETURNS

A word's like a body part you almost feel.

Have one like a ribbon up your throat.

×

Bury it. Dig it up. Chew on it. Repeat.
Dactyl. Dactyl. Dactyl. Iamb.
Trochee. Trochee. Trochee. Trochee.

×

Bruised to stay in time a while, but not so fast,
all prelude full of thoughts to have gotten away:

twenty-some-odd hours in a hot, gray house
mumbling, "Tank cars drag graffiti through the hay."

WHEN RHYME FAILS RHYME

ATTEMPTS TO COME TO THE RESCUE

As it happens, my failures, which are most of what happens,
are like my having collapsed on stage but with the curtain down.

Some of them, though, are like having, with a touch,
knocked over a huge imaginative structure to which

I've been adding for what feels like years.
So I lie with myself, unsure how long I've been here:

curtains and furniture, clouds that build and cling.
Hard up for wet blossoms, more trivia slithers in,

music gets easily confused again with place,
and only not living forever is all that's the case.

TWO POEMS OF TWENTY LINES EACH

I. NAP JERK WITH F TRAIN

In my phone and sort of knowing where the sun was,
my crushed double finished work that I'd begun.
The day'd bored into me; every song went "like this."
I practiced many a removal. You could've said I was a van.
And there was almost more to life, the money out there
gaping, a much-elated dread that even theory won't forbid,
and in the light-soaked scene of online banking,
my inner voice of prudence left out principled language—
all prudence all the time, a virtue possessed by grass
and by rats—and if its sentences touched one another
like states, they touched *me* that way, too; they programmed.

Imagined at large, the world was more ward than field,
and as I slept for real, I saw the achingest scene—
Saint Paul headless, Saint Peter still clutching his keys—
and then the blanched car's abstraction like a print's third pull,
its impulsive disabling of my reverie, of me,
to which I said "Which future? What's above this?"
before I uncraved and then pretended not to've moved,
the woman across from me screaming to her friend,
"He has this truly awful laugh but they're in love!"

II. INJURIES

I heard someone who'd once hurt me
had slipped, had fallen on the stairs
down to Bergen Street station
and broken terribly some vertebrae,
and in my gasping at this fact, my breath
came back, for just an instant, as happiness,
and then I wanted to die from shame, a shame
it seemed could really only be achieved
by way of the end of some world.

And yet to think of the end of a world
is to think of those who *might* have lived in it,
and I knew that we had seen close up
the world they'll never see, a bright mess
we'd put in our heads first, yes—
the leaves all green, the sky its blue best—
and thereby put our lives in shapes
that lives aren't meant to take, our bodies
just numbers, a look in our eyes
that made our minds take on water, a love
like having screamed at being moved.

SMALL BEFORE-CHURCH POEM

Laughing at the thought of lack
of pleasure as a pleasure—
monuments not yet objects,
a waltz not for dancing but for labor—

and having slogged through pollen,
considerable weeds and fallen
power lines to be here, I have more
to say about this day than of the year.

Blasphemy's part of the Logos too,
like wanting the light my way. Towers
disappear into their bells and never argue.
An apple holds its peace and wets a nail.

THE ID

My tar's as warm as the rich in winter,
and having binge-watched nature
and been binged on by it, I,
intangible, go off half-camouflaged,
as happens when I edit a sentence for clarity,
thereby muddling what was there,
and grieve your missing out on April's air's
absurd flourishes, reality's trickle
and flood cranked up to pattern,
your forced smile's dimmest gibberish
ready to have to punctuate and change
what you say when I say, "You thrill at filth,"
or when again you fend away
this disappointingly bright bright morning.

KALININGRAD, FORMERLY KÖNIGSBERG

Full of cloud changes, ghost-of looks, rocks, recalled
talk, a snuffbox, Kant's walks continue nameless,
just stills, not films, filed back there in the dream realm:
same tunnel, different light; the year a bit behind itself;
"You won't be able to find that there," my intermittent claim.
There are three imaginations: one nascent, one useful,
and the last without hope, though there are more,
of course (or there should be), but for now let's limit it—
my prose could use some work—to only three.

A name that would serve this city's evening's needs
is darkness's emptier synonym were it to have one.
The suggestion and bother I'm so often at home in—
they're never what I didn't mean, the game I'll later
deny ever having played, the most undopeawayable
of pains, its shine, the quiet shapes that ride behind it
I can never quite recede enough to see in their entirety,
their being always a call to the edge of what I am,
if I'm one figure in one vast, inhabited painting.

I WON'T BE LONG

I play I'm the same, but I change
the way a sky might on days

it doesn't seem to, flailing around
as if I've failed somehow to make

out to you a thing or two, you
who tell me more than "That's the year."

×

I'm here until I'm made the break
in meaning I turn away from

out of a bitter love of time
and all the sounds it carries in me,

words that come from just one
face over from my own . . .

×

Odds were I'd not take part in this,
but now what else

to be blessed with save for a name.

NIGHTINGALELESSNESS

Lack of nostalgia / felt as nostalgia—

once just a taste,
that's now the daily mouth,

and mirrors are older than bread.

Near to a thought
that's not yet cooled to truth—

that's one way to live, or half of one,

but what's its knowledge like?
Like touch? Like reading? Like sleep?

Why, in other words,

or in cubes of wet neon on dirt,
the one face?

And why's the other unlooked upon, into, for?

Everyone who's dead's now "problematic"—
leave that out of this.

You're where you write not fading into traffic.

But that rumor's always attached to here
is absolutely capital—you hear

of a bird; you hear, in fact, a bird.

A few hours blocked the day,
and in the meantime, you got that way,

or this, and then rushed to curtail a view.

A little sunlight on
and then eventually through

your eyelids boots your body up,

and with that, at little last,
the spasm into what you're going to do.

Come high bright noon

and come the corollary thorn,
you're going to sit right down

and write yourself a flower you can sing when you're sad

but you'll be glad when you sing,
your songs instanced by the looks of things

now lost in some fire or fires

and so weightless as the best of spires,
a cumulus of what you hunt

and of how what you hunt haunts

and so hunts you back,
its ghost so many demoed amens.

Being—not staying—the course is the trouble;

places yet to be, opportunities to grieve,
a strangely damaging wind around

your city that serves, in a world young or lapsed,

as something like a budding grove's inverse,
thus adding blame to bliss, you've stopped somewhere

but think pains to keep moving the aforesaid social hole along,

the poem or the song that never knows how dead,
dead or not, you are (or how gone)

and then makes its only sounds until it fades—

again
(like a worm in a church does)

again

again
again—

and then sticks out your blood.

FORWARD SLASH

When I've lived too late in my life and everyone else's,
about the sun, in the end, I'll do anyway what ice does—
stays if it must, or goes—and I'll expect the outdoors
but get instead a room, along with the "is"
in "missing," the "in" in "forgetting," a few feelings
believed in, but just beside the point of having with ease,
with speed, seen pieces of what can't happen, ideas
so fast that only years, if that, could get them back please.

STAR TURN

That the deepest wound is the least unique
surprises nobody but the living.
Secretly, and with what feels like good reason,
we're the pain the people we love
put the people they no longer love in.

SPECIFICS

To make bruiseless
moves at night because
I've made wood memory.

×

To hear screams
as experiments
at songs from too much.

×

To see life coming
and to go with you
into it (death, too)

and to not see a corpse
or what's before it
as nutritious.

×

To sound other than
the way (any way) that this
computer sounds.

HET GOUDEN HOF

Let it be said
we bided time

with our boots on,
and on occasion

with them off.

The barman goes over
the drinks in anxious French;

a child describes
a jet's two silent lines.

$\times$

(Big deal the pitch increases as the glass fills.)

(So what the same thing happens with a cup.)

$\times$

So what the day's
dressed hastily,

as even tangles
have results

and are results,
a flustered garden.

10 July 2016 / Olsene

GRACE HARTIGAN'S KITE

But one sign of evening in the late afternoon,
an insect creaks and scrapes in the grass,
unsusceptible to voices like this one
or others, and far from any city's stacks of logic.
Weirdly clean, forever overhanging matter,
at first I trust, at last, in color, and sleep-skate letters
into he who—thrown the floor (or better)
and too out to feel, so well lit as to be invisible—
manages life that's otherwise this side of the go-ahead
that darkness gives (or mild violence)
as when a mostly daily stranger
puts a coffee or the paper in my hand,
the familiar just globs of psychology,
maybe, and so about to be studied away . . .
Things can be measured in two
of two ways: according to their nature
or according to an accident they possess.
"Wither anonymity," I say, moving on unexplained—
my own eyes in a mirror after having watched a fight,
strong winds destroying Grace Hartigan's kite—
but one sign of evening in the late afternoon.

NO EXPECTATIONS

Obscure's

the scene I said—
it heard me.

(I've grown old

again, or I've
never grown old.)

Next I said

I said fade to faded
black, reflect

an averageness

goes on refusing,
is thrown

absurdly down

and back
to pebble, flower,

polyp, pin drop—

and said it in words
for a box.

Sleep

turns me in and,
love aside,

what's left?

Sleep turns
me in and love

aside.

Q & A

You asked where I get my ideas, and I'd just like to say,
and this is really more of a comment than an answer,
but I've been thinking a lot about brain surgery lately,

and I'd give my right brain for a box for to haul
my ideas a little less than halfway across the country
so that they could be unceremoniously dumped into the Pacific,

but—and here's the rub—that's also the part of me
that just loves to come home to a vase of azaleas
and to drop all my coins and my keys into a dumb little dish.

NOW BUT NEVER

I mind
the glow,

ignore

the flag's
wriggle.

I can't

not live
with you.

×

I am I
because I'm why

I can't even

have nice things—
some business light

through loosest shade,

my blood's voice down
the thicket;

an instant year

lived mostly lost
and inwardly,

not laughed with.

I USED TO PUT THINGS PAST ME

Maybe hell is in fact

very quiet, is a hell
you can tell the value of.

Maybe animals come

to forgive one another,
and that's what's called time.

×

Today though, today

lets a cloud go
empty, and long

after afternoon,

a look at what
could come about

and won't.

POEM TO MY DAUGHTER

The sky has, *is*, one exit, one excuse,
and if I'm dead now that I'm saying this,
I can't vouch for my transition from life
as having been rough or even evident.
Have I tried turning it off and then on again?
Have I tried throwing it against the wall?
Getting to know you, getting to know all
about you getting the mirror to mean
not only me, and thinking I must look
dumber than I look—dumber, then, than prose—
I walk through the laundry room regretting
getting the weekend done this way, as if
backstage, and say the name of your birthplace
as if I'd lost a hundred dollars there,
which I may have . . . Dear, when nowhere, don't do
as those of us in nowhere do—just go.

TWENTY-FOUR HOURS FROM HOME

Where, Ms. Bishop, should the boy and I be today?
All precedent's out of the question, the question
out of something like itself and lacking answer.

What we have here's here as if it starts at the skin—
a siren's cruel looping, a new phrase in mid-use;
saved message: his sister's wild crooning to her doll.

Save for the getting home, our travels are over,
so we're putting it all back in our bags with talk
of birds above a river in a sketch by Turner,

an imaginary church interior filled
with virtue's matchless purple, and a battlefield
of late-July grass, unvisited and ochre.

Elsewhere this dry summer, tight flowers in the dust,
I lost myself to river, cellar, debt, self, sea;
I did a thing that comforts when it's done too much

because of loneliness, a fact all people know,
and none—whether of brain of youth or brain of age—
can understand as well as color-killing sun.

The technical in shreds, a Doberman saunters
toward its owner's open hand, and there we have it—
all that happens by a seed's end, a Saturday—

and maybe now we'll feel what time is,
our images going and coming like ashes; a city
and citizens named for one another after water.

The conquered moon'll pale alone, and soon enough
knit hats will morph our shadows into minarets,
while secretless mysteries gag the whole of space.

Mostly, though, that falters, and people stride freely,
the snow on a few of them branded as grace,
the rain on others thought of only as unlucky.

A NATURE FOR MY PICTURE

While it just so happens I'm believed to be
aligned with me—that is, I've been black-boxed
most properly—the resolve to get closer's a desire
to turn back, and having barely avoided having
never even been, I'd prefer a star's disastrous middle
to some dull and bearable love's high treacle.
(Now sit back, relax, and watch specifics roll in
with all the intimacies of sentences, of sieves.)
The mind-body problem isn't the neck, unless it is,
and our dice seem cast as prices these days,
except when they're not, as when a thought incites
a single frame into a nest of them, thus adding parasite
to path, a thrown rock's wake in a plate-glass window
to a thrown rock scattering minnows.

Here comes death, leaving pieces of us anywhere;
Edward Hopper probably had this, too,
to paint about: her somehow defiant in her leafing
through some book, him somehow submissive in his eating.
Even adults know I'm not right, am hell, and yet
you've taken such good notes around me, nature,

not fumbling—how could you have?—
in all this latest wind. Alive, for now,
in the de facto always-has-been, and error-haired,
in shoes and clothes outrageous for my mood,
I'm over the game again, like trying not to change
somebody's mind about a word. Aghast,
love asks after me, its tongue justly colorless,
having not in the least—imagine *that*!—reversed its loss.

FIELD DAY

To say the butcher's fouled apron's good painting seems wrong.
To say the butcher's fouled apron's a garden *is* wrong.

Desire's your one honey, every augur's double bummer,
but to burn all wonder isn't *your* job, it's money's—
torch you carry, torch you throw—and this time money
feels like chasing id and ego, each on a differently televised beach,
one in color, the other in giant and terrifying white,
while hanging out in touch is something kind of like what thought is:

the opposite of money, which is change (pun lived with)
or for one definition of "interest" to have vanished.
It's okay then? To want that? To just go ahead and stop?
Sound like guns out in the crops: slight discomfort, hard return.
You're beyond neither you nor any death you don't expect,

and better still is to have quit this in a prior extra life
as if you're new again now, as if it's *real* that you *are*,
as a song ends sentences sooner than you think it should,
its words on your brain's lowest branch, whatever happens,
wherever else they put themselves, the sun gearing into the grass
today's ask of the weather, the recto, the verse.

Bird trips sensor, noise spooks bird, and what you know now's that those
are only *mock* guns out in the crops. Hallelujah, peace be with you,
as you were as it were: surrounded by the work you thought
you'd thought your way out of (*worked* your way out of)
by thinking in *their* thought while *they* thought in *yours*—

here a code, there a code, everywhere a code, code
shrieking like a diamond ploughing cash-machine glass.

LOST POEM

The quantity
I bow to

when coached
into the crowd

is just my own—

one cloud (or flower)
already like

the rest but not
the one good jewel.

×

I told myself
remember where

you put it and
I know I know

what "it" was

but I can't recall
what "where" was—

the trouble,
just as well.

CHARMED, I'M SURE

Me first.

You first.

Shotgun.

Not it.

$\times$

One question:
why can I care?

$\times$

Sincere despair's
a dark
back vowel,

one else in a room
in a house that's there

for now.

GRAVE OF MIND

Three's the start of evening in December in the north;
come end of June, three marks the thick of afternoon.
Shadows mention branches as they can in any month,
and "friend" can share a phrase with "owes me money,
pictures," the sky the fragile edge around a sentence
that's the day. Not for worlds, the one world all at once:
well-lit runways, slums, the past before us like a future,
that song about a mansion on the hill. You know where
I'm going with this—a beer with dinner, scars and cramped
diaries proving history's not impossible—as memory's ramps
and ducts and galleries, its halls of imposture, make love
no less perverse than any economic model, my having
moved through forms of feeling seeming close to not living,
like being used to being afraid or being made a federal case of.

Of course the oranged-up morning found me particled awake,
doubt gray, the rather awkward thought that ivy'd spread
(I'd done nothing whatsoever that I knew of to be rid of it)
staying on for several minutes then becoming just dreamt,
a blurred reversal, a way to put mute worry to me cruelly,
confusedly, while bands of cold around the Earth secured

appearances in alleys like demesnes between words' textures
icing over every corner of the reader-listener's maze.
And that's fine, that's what I'd figured. Or is it? Or was it?
There's only too much nature, pure and dirty—some loam
and grass and little piles of our initial ash, no derision in them,
all brainlessly distant and varied like meanings or seasons or shit—
and there's a bitter severed head in sawdust plotting, sinning,
that stares into the hour it seems it's been since it's been anything.

ANNIVERSARY

Having tired of the song I've been listening to's
like being punched for doing what I'm asked to do,
and it gets so that it gets to where music's time itself—
there, but empty, the peace before the phone rings,
a huge clean gape to be spoiled by opposing dreams.
As a joke, I should feel bright, walk back along roads
where I've been uselessly sad, throw the whole works
into the drink, all the better to think on what I've heard.
The effective world, the dead one, wants through us,
a coincidence (wording's chances of being otherwise
being good) I almost never call still living here,
though I go to come back—we're both a little like that:
expressions that stay when the new ones are made,
two scars that keep stretching with the skin they're on.

THE PAINT NEED BE REAL

or so the painting
complains—

its dreams in swarms,

a *sic*
at every strikethrough;

for years half-touched and hacked

back into glances;
a this, a that,

a the other thing churning in dirt.

×

Surprise!
—still more

to feel there,

a right
word

not unimaginably

not
that far away.

after Roger Raveel's Koren en witte rechthoek, *1968–1988*

COUNTDOWN

Let's go then, you and me . . . 3 . . .
—this gauze collecting blood, the midday heat
still in the concrete, a tetchy spider stop-
motioning its way along a table—
in a direction to be named later, the this-
is-this-house-and-another mode of dream
just up ahead of us; the look, sound, smell, feel,
and taste of missing out on sense behind.
We'll like it there: people live longer—
or maybe it just seems like that,
the light on the floor of a room at a time
of year not really remembered as such;
the nowhere of the new, theorization of which
is pointless and perverse, like mocking an animal,
as memory changes everything, then cages it.
The blood that's left in us might be its own shadow,
the kind that makes the ground look both wet
and not there, but there's no ground in us,
our many breaths thus far successes (see above),
and if we're "subject" we're just grateful to've been painted.

It's okay going away under colors like these,
and we'll want to say that those were dimmer times;
that what yesterday were our ears' convolutions
sitting tight in minds no longer gaps nor ghosts
are today those minds' rats, which is to say,
strangely, that to own one's own gait or cadence
is like trying to get one's own attention
from the other side of an upturned squad car;
that what we want from song is for song—
or for the note before a song's first note—
to give us more than we could want from song;
that what we want from summer . . . 2 . . . is just
to pour some middling whiskey over hail.
We've mirror-fed our sleep-bruised faces, our selves
craving, caving in, as though mouths or hands
had closed in our chests—we should know: we drank alone
and talked enough—and let me guess: something's
ruined so we're buying a new one, the paged life
of the sky above these neighborhoods' Venn diagram
being all we've ever known of demand and supply?

Were we put here to know not coming back?
I'd say so. But maybe "held here" or "left here"
is far more to the point. Brief cloud cover, a pause
between chords, a shock that in retrospect
won't register as such, but that at the time seems

blissfully mortifying, as when someone who reads
"Missed Connections" just for pleasure suddenly
finds himself summoned by a not-so-total stranger—
these are what we'd rather believe in. And after
a sequence of frequent secret outbursts, when what we fear
the most, even after we've long grown bored of our fears,
gets gussied back up as progress conquering its opposite,
we'll do our long division in the dirt with a stick
and think until we sleep until, still sleeping, we see
we've missed out on something forcedly historic—
several vintage stamps stuck to a circuit board, say,
or fascists not gagging on swigs of crushed glass.
The reverse of not feeling like it—now we know
we had to seem like that then, but when this alley's done
clutching the sun . . . I . . . we quit squinting and live.

COLLECTED POEMS

Right back at all this now not enough for me,
back to out of purpose into up against the empty,
today's shame's gawking over dead grass at traffic—
is remorse whatever the clean brain says it is?
My sentiments exactly like some others:
why not? Big contrition's long hello: how bother?
It's a draggy life, really, in a tolerable code,
and one of these years, and as late as I like,
I'll walk back across the quicksand,
get right with never being any good.
Made to feel like I'm not in the room with you
or like I'm around but not worth looking into,
blurred as old music that's explained as it's heard,
I'll need a throat down which to cram back every word.

REMAINERS

Don't you remember being young, when language was magic without meaning?
—TONI MORRISON

Do we possess Thursday? —KESTON SUTHERLAND

When I went out to kill myself
I thought only the world
could possibly be more thorough—
hear me out, miracle,
my first first sentence in a year—
and soon thereafter felt
not loved exactly, but dreamt of,
and called up afternoons
that in their moments had meaning,
along with some others
that had only vague presence,
and then, having looked death
in the forehead and fetched the mail,
used a gently used book
(*The Bereaved Parent*, a volume
mistakenly sent me
by a bookstore in Omaha
instead of *Short Letter*,

Long Farewell, which I had wanted
to give to my brother)
to move some dog shit from my lawn
into a Safeway bag
that had snagged in a nearby tree,
the small cough of a broom
along concrete a few doors down,
one of the many sounds
my life gives off, and what's useful
is real—or so I thought—
but having now flown many miles
to say my poetry
in a kind of corporate rec room,
I quarter-heartedly
reach for a pint glass in the dark
of an old friend's guest room
and spill cold water on—among
other guest things—my phone,
my good shoes, my duffel . . .
fuck it: can I start this over
with someone else's throat?

×

Was that vomit or a speech scroll,
a *tractatus* or scraps?
Less is the same; a fossil gives
good sample and is dead.

There at the hole in everything,
I won't have what I'd known:
the filth of light a city seen
from air at midnight is,
the nouns you thought to use because
I'm very close to gone.
Another's mind is like the bottom
of a boat half run aground,
and veiled so as to be seen, all dreams
are first last looks around.
New instincts (no doubt speech was one)
must feel at first like smears
along the length of any sense.
Bird noise, bird noise, backspace—
the laziest activist wraps
himself in CAUTION tape
and walks into the evening-orange
disorders of the surf.
What is it with the end? It moves
from mouth to mouth, a word.
There's not much else to do but fall
or fuss about subjects
and objects, as in what if when
I close these eyes, all light
has been extinguished or
just hasn't yet been devised?
And people—our looks and feelings

and thoughts; the things our thoughts
produce, and the things that neither
we nor what we think
have anything to do with making
(e.g., the range of any morning);
and lastly, if not finally,
that drabbest of mysteries:
the block on offering content,
any content at all,
to being one person, on pain
of a relapse into god-talk—
all this the poem threatens
to put to music and/or worse.
To breathe's not chosen, mostly,
though there's another way
to look at it, which is to say
that it's the only thing
we nearly always choose to do,
except when we're swimming
underwater or feigning death
or, for awful or else,
when we decide to drop ourselves.
Back to from where I came,
my having been here is behind
my having headed that way,
so why not call me eternity

with a chance of Thursday
with a chance your scare paragraph
will adhere to the grid?
Eyes unaware of one another,
each with somewhere to be,
I'd like to think it wasn't me
who went vertiginous,
but rather some six-year-old girl
who of her own accord
began spinning in a scorched-out yard
and never really stopped.
I might get to February,
the hard lake like a field,
the field like the last shred of Earth.
A shadow's no object,
a shadow's a situation,
just one weightless facet
of moving out into a day.
"Your skull is beautiful"
doesn't mean "I feel peculiar,"
although it points to what
seem like passed catastrophes,
lenses cleaned back to grit.
But first I was and all that blood—
a whole orchard of blood
or something very much like it—

slow liquid ignoring
my reflections in its motions,
which passed and then collapsed
immediately into feeling
and then *really* away,
the way the whole way of us will.
Now's an age I'm of two minds
not to praise, even and especially as
I'm praising it for real,
as real, all hell coalescing
just like it always has,
like a house I'd need keys to leave.
Night in, night in, night in,
songs rush darkly through my insides
as any disease might—
a point is that which has no part,
a line is breadthless length—
while some of what I feel or see
sails out to where it's heard.
Nothing, poem or otherwise,
is of such quality
that there's no one who could hate it
down to normal only dead.
Labor and happenstance, time's glass,
and maybe thought hates me
as it moves about what makes it,

though I'm not a person
on whom the many occasions
that go by the name of
what it is I've turned away from
make little impression,
a far-off flock resembling smoke,
for one; the null feeling
"Happy New Year" is a question.
Explosively lonely—
as though my head were made simply
to weigh my tongue and teeth—
because a doctor in the hall
pushed past me in anger
(so maybe I got in her way),
I'm ninety-nine years old,
the only of my friends to not
have dropped and disappeared.
Kindness's numerous sorrows
keep me almost honest,
and gray with life, adrift among
all evidence, I know
how to know I'm still here: a schedule
crumpled on a bus seat,
words hurled weatherward—these are news
from a collective place,
or at the very least they're news

from a place we *could* share,
although no notarized paper says so,
nor does any chiseled stone.
A fed-up blue jay having fled it,
a branch perfects its shake,
and I've the right to look at light
that reflects off your teeth.
The fraught way a thinking body
eats into its clear need
to fail with thoughts of tomorrow's
not proof of existence
(that said, the facts of failure are)
and this is where I claim
that I don't fear disappearing,
but only my being here
dying, not really following
any of anything—
going once, going, and that's it.
Empire fades like a taste
or many tastes—and brutally—
its spoken-for glamour
crossing over into quiet
that's as spent as spent gets
this verdigris non-century,
not necessarily
to anyone's ears, you hear me?

(I'll never grasp so much
as I assume I'm saying now.)
Write something sometime
in my cremains with your finger,
a vague line you'd like, like
Made as if unremarked as air.
Today, though, sit with me,
I want to give you this bookmark,
print from years ago shoved between
two pages of some tome
about Minnesota plant life
(or placed there with much care—
who am I to say, as I'd've
been only a small child
at the time, and hardly compelled
by states or their flora):

LIGHTS ALL ASKEW IN THE HEAVENS

———

Stars Not Where They Seemed or
Were Calculated to be but
Nobody Need Worry.

The sky the sky in theory, jest,
I struggle to be glad,
and in the other other hand,

your poem for no good
reason, in itself confounded—
skip past the end: you'll find
I've died and do many dead things—
it makes living waver.
Ahead of day's informations,
you speak your every sentence
both warily and carelessly,
as one might grip a fish
that one has planned to gut and eat.
Their first designs feel right,
but somehow there isn't enough
hard crying in their sounds,
so you mouth on as if talking
were not its own drawback,
which it is when done the wrong way
or when done very well.
(I've coughed the halves of Monday's pills
from the spoon of my hand.)
Red sky on bad TV tonight
on furniture, on skin—
I'll memorize it like it was
yesterday somewhere else,
like I was a different woman
who'd done time in a park
where pink repeating petals were

birthed at the crowd and were
transferable from mind to mind
as patched contrivances.
(She liked Old Fitzgerald bourbon
and was legally blind.
I remember she tried to read.)
The single return on
becoming adult, the one
justice in forgoing
a sphere of possibility,
is the reception of
reality—at once the pain
and balm in the only fact
of the onliest realm:
that it exists, and I in it
this Thursday afternoon.
Everything's coming down ruptures,
awry, very much like
when I pretend money can't buy
sordid excellence as,
say, Sarasota or Vegas
or Ashland, Oregon.
Life, like shock, is temporary,
and even near its close,
this life had best pass for itself,
although I've nothing much

with which to menace it today,
June rain going the way
of handwritten letters, low clouds.
Heavy now, I barely feel it,
and there are rumors that
I'll hold this posture, the loose sense,
in other words, that thought—
rid of texture, as what I said
was mirrored on water—
begins and ends as needed.
Put yet another way,
consciousness's heel on thought's wing—
one doesn't learn it's there
until it's made its way elsewhere,
forever not knowledge
and certainly never a thing.
All the world's a warning—
it just goes away to show you
there's no paltrier year
than the year you think you get good.
(Go ahead, compare death
to rest one last time—it can't hurt.)
In a place devoid of
or made wholly of novelty
(watch me brighten over
to a garden now and void this)

the heart's ramparts chorus,
all sociology explodes,
as if I'd known thousands
of dialects, but not the sounds
of water over ice,
and whatever I have to say
for myself, I'll soon hand over,
at prolonged last, to you.
Credible thrones are few,
I get that, and architecture's
gift for fiction's as true
as a day's being paraphrased,
necessarily so,
so I know I've had done with it.
Waking threatens the dream
with material—that champagne
I sipped from a Ziploc
never was, though it could have been
and could yet be the case.
Face facing down, sun on the ground,
some otherworldly wind—
here I can infiltrate, for now,
the ready emptiness
through which all vision has to swim.
I used to think my eyes
would feel like something close to new

when I could see for myself
the pictured floors of distant rooms,
but so does everyone
(rows of dots in dust on those floors—
they were all there before,
and yet only in a story;
and in that story was
an orchid, and in that orchid
dust, and in that dust
still one more story with an orchid
et goddamn cetera)
and in the first known photograph
in which humans appear,
one person shines another's shoes.
In so many still lifes
the sense that someone was just there
is mostly what is felt,
yet one piece of fruit seems to have
come open of itself
for some reason, many, or none.
When there cease to be
or there are only pleasant weathers,
love poetry, so called,
will be the only poetry,
and it will have to be
enough for us, while also not

being nearly enough
so as to still be poetry.
I hear it for—and from—
my memory, that heavy limb
that promises its way
around history, the problem,
disappearing the halls
where it sets up its lamps, its beams,
its impromptu mirrors
(crosses opposite one another
for one weird example)
some difficult to see as such,
and why not dwell on that,
or better yet rehash belief?
I may have days still to live,
but there's a trouble under mind,
some combination of
irrational variety,
interest, and faint alarm.
About to be unfeasible,
an acrobat of ash,
I am become how I'm ending:
slowly; it becomes me—
the game that all these remnants are,
this negligent triumph
like a sleep.

A NOTE AND SOME ACKNOWLEDGMENTS

As usual, many of the poems in this book borrow, bend, fold, spindle, and mutilate language from other sources. Liner notes with regard to such things seem to me beside the point, but I'd like to mention that the title "Grave of Mind" comes from Laura (Riding) Jackson's "Intelligent Prayer."

Some of the poems in this book have been published previously, often in pieces, in different versions, and/or with different titles. My thanks to the editors of *Cloud Rodeo*, *Copper Nickel*, *Critical Quarterly*, *The Fanzine*, *Gramma*, *Harper's*, *The Nation*, *The New Republic*, *Oversound*, *Ploughshares*, *A Public Space*, *The Spectacle*, *Visible Binary*, *Wag's Review*, *Washington Square*, *Web Conjunctions*, and the Academy of American Poets Poem-a-Day series.

Thanks also to the University of Denver Office of Internationalization and the Baltic Writing Residency.

Lastly, I thank Éireann Lorsung and Jonathan Vanhaelst, without whom this book would not exist.

BORN IN KNOXVILLE, TENNESSEE IN 1970 AND RAISED
IN EAU CLAIRE, WISCONSIN, GRAHAM FOUST IS
DIRECTOR OF UNDERGRADUATE STUDIES IN ENGLISH
AND LITERARY ARTS AT THE UNIVERSITY OF DENVER.